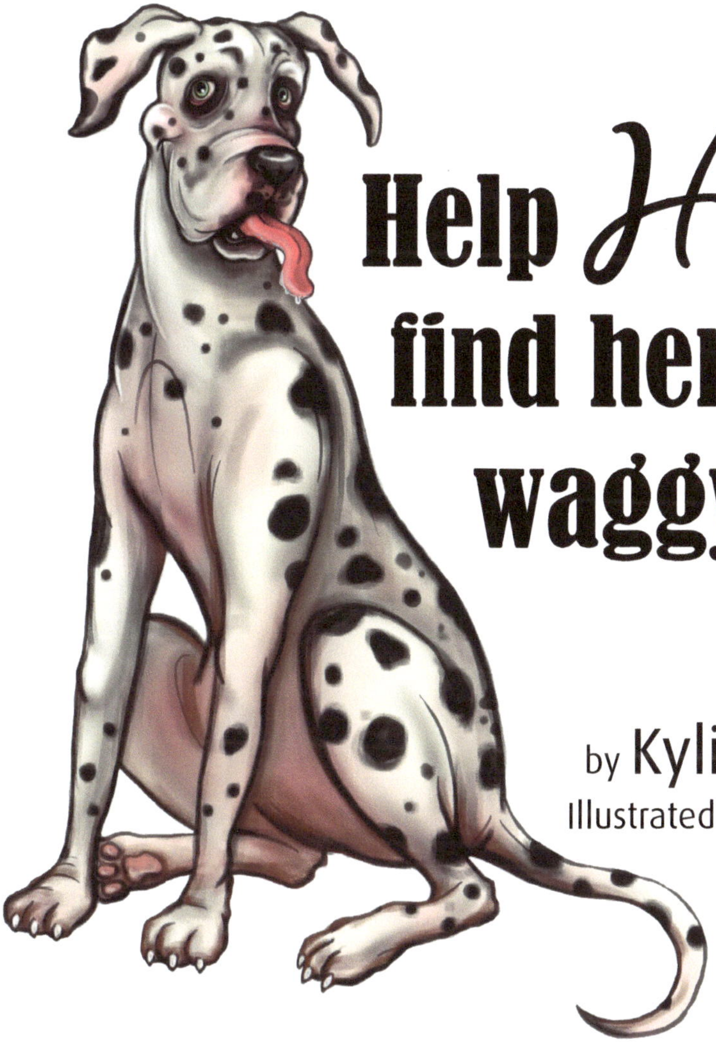

Help Hope find her waggy tail

by Kylie Symons
Illustrated by Brittany Alcorn

www.alysbooks.com
Your Book | Our Mission

Help Hope Find Her Waggy Tail

Copyright © Kylie Symons
Illustration copyright © Brittany Alcorn

First Edition 2015
Published by Aly's Books

www.alysbooks.com
Your Book | Our Mission

Edited by Irrefutable Proof
www.irrefutable-proof.com

Designed by Fish Biscuit
fishbiscuitdesign.com.au

All rights reserved. No part of this book may be reproduced or transmitted in any form or by any means, electronic, mechanical, photocopying or otherwise without the prior permission of the publisher.

ISBN: 978 0 9941767 9 0

Dedicated to the most amazing rescue dog I have ever known, Hope, and her rescuers, Kerrie and Kayla from Puppy Tales Rescue.

'To my hubby Brett, thank you for always encouraging me to follow my dreams!
To my funny, spunky son Lachlan, thank you for your love of books and loving my character Hope!
To my angel in heaven, Isabelle, thank you for bringing Puppy Tales into my life through Sweety, and for making me want to be a better person and Mumma!'

I'm a Great Dane, that's a type of dog.

I'm very big, with floppy ears, a long tongue and a tail that doesn't wag.

I live in a small pen where my owners make me have lots of puppies.

But they take them away when they are still very little to sell in pet shops.

This makes me very sad.

My owners don't look after me very well, so that's why my tail doesn't wag anymore.

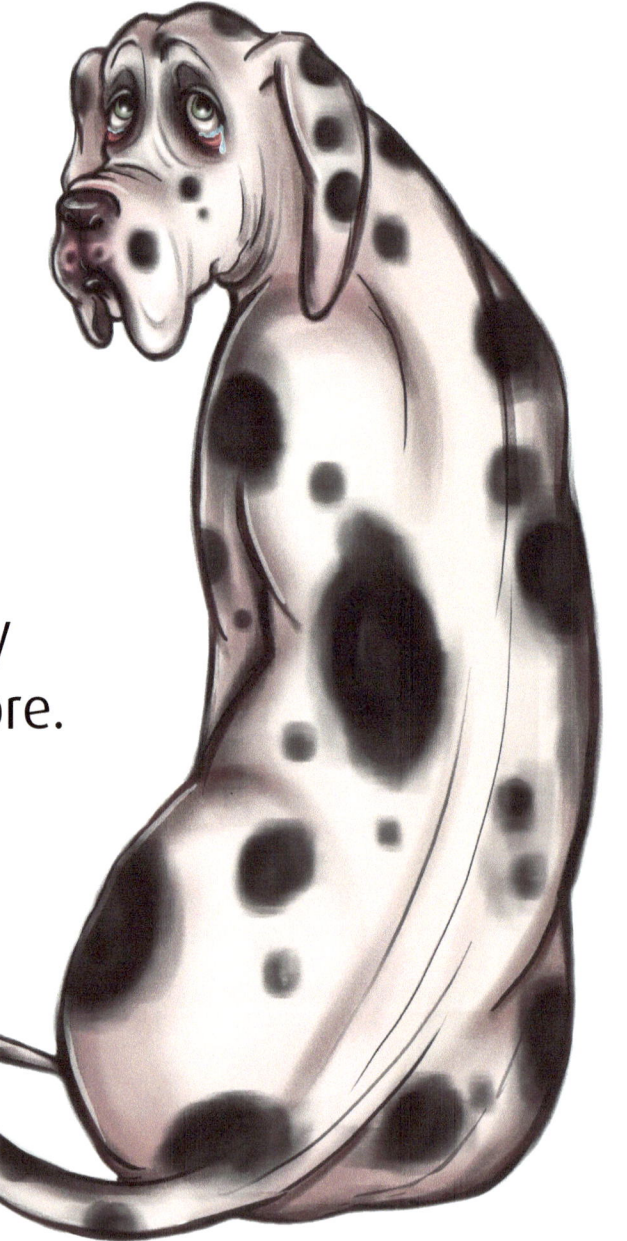

I want a nice home where my owners love me and my tail wags all day long!

Do you think you could help me find my happy, waggy tail?

I have a food bowl but it is empty...
What should be in my bowl?

Yes! Dog Food!

That makes my tail wag!

My water bowl is green and slimy...

What should my water bowl look like?

Yes! Clean and clear, with fresh water.

That makes my tail wag!

I don't have anywhere to sleep...
Where should I sleep?

Yes! In a soft, comfy dog kennel.

That makes my tail wag!

I smell and I'm very dirty...

What should I have?

Yes! A nice soapy bath!

That makes my tail wag!

I'm always stuck in this little pen...
Where can I go?

Yes! On a nice long walk.

That makes my tail wag!

I'm feeling a little sick...
Where should I be taken?

Yes! To the vets to make me feel better.

That makes my tail wag!

I have an itchy back but I can't scratch it...

What do I need?

Yes! A good scratchy pat.

That makes my tail wag!

I don't have a name...

What do you think my name should be?

Yes! That's right I should be called *Hope*.

That really makes my tail wag!

Do you know what I want more than all of these things?

I want someone to rescue me so I can find a nice family who will give me a happy waggy tail forever!

What kind of animal would you like to rescue?

Draw your animal in the frame.

Notes for Teachers

Before reading

Ask your students if they have a pet at home – discuss their pets and the things they do to look after those pets. Talk about the similarities and differences in needs between the different kinds of pets. Talk about the different places you can get a pet from (breeders, pet stores, friends/family, rescue centres etc.).

Introduce the concept of a 'puppy farm' and why it's so unpleasant – an age appropriate picture showing such a place may be useful and help consolidate understanding.

After reading questions and activities

Why is Hope sad at the start of the story? Do you think it's ok that Puppy Farms exist? Why/Why not?

What were some of the things mentioned in the story that made Hope happier? Can you think of any other things that might make her happy? Children can brainstorm with a partner or in a small group.

Have you ever seen anyone being mean to an animal? What were they doing and how do you think the animal was feeling at the time?

Draw a picture of yourself with a pet you would like to have one day. Think about the things you could do to keep it happy and healthy.

Show the class illustrations of animals in different situations (having a bath, getting a pat, tied up on a short chain, in a small cage, being hit with a stick, chasing a ball) and have the children talk about how the animals might be feeling in these situations.

Going further

Arrange to visit a rescue centre/animal shelter if available. Arrange for children to assist with caring of animals.

Discuss whether you think it would be better to buy your pet from a pet store or from a rescue shelter. Guide this discussion so they understand the importance of rescuing animals in shelters. Older children could be introduced to the idea that buying animals like puppies from a pet store keeps these puppy farms running, which isn't good.

Organise a local veterinary or rescue centre worker to visit the classroom. They can speak with the children about responsible pet ownership and share (age appropriate) stories of animals they have rescued.

In small groups, make a poster that encourages people to rescue an animal or just be kind to animals. Teachers can provide ideas for simple slogans/messages such as 'animals have feelings too', and they can be printed out ready for younger children to stick onto posters rather than write their own.

Discuss ideas of other things you could do by yourself or as a class to help animals (eg. build a bird feeder to place outside, adopt a wild animal through WWF, Australia Zoo or any of the other organisations that run such programs).

https://www.facebook.com/PuppyTalesRescue

http://www.oscarslaw.org/

https://www.petrescue.com.au/

http://www.halrescue.org/AWE.html

http://www.humanesociety.org/parents_educators/lesson_plans_for_teachers.html

http://www.rspca.org.au/campaigns/puppy-farms

https://www.petfinder.com/pro/for-shelters/lesson-plan-caring-dog/

Dedications

Lachlan Aaron Symons and Isabelle Amelia Symons
Jade and baby
Stella, Joy, Scott, Max and Wallace Carter
Chloe Rider
Jordan Douglas Fullwood
Caleb David and Shamini-Rose Osman
Sienna and Riley Belshaw
Laycee and Noaah
Lily Beth Ann Seevers
Riley James Plummer
Leitchville Kindergarten
Gunbower Kindergarten
Church Family
Reba, Minnie and Buddy
Homeless Hounds and Second Chance Animal Rescue
Stephanie Sheridan Burns and Payton Louise Burns
William and Ella
Snoopy and Ang
Karla and Ella
Zannon
Bella and Ruby
Oscar
Blakey
Kippa
Altona Meadows Kindergarten
Emma McLean Kindergarten
Carlo and Ruby Sartinas
Carlton Gardens Primary School
Oreo, Buddy and Jaxon R D Lewis
Snoopy and Miz

Jessie, Sam, Luna, Coco, Kitty and Princess
Cindy Alcorn
Tyler Aitchison
Rylan and Hendrik
Anne & Fred Church
Molly Meha and Jack Patterson
Kate Maree Shaw
Dana, Batman and Poppy
Dozer (Hope's daughter)
Terri Earley and Charlotte
Krissy Dudgeon and Amanda Dudgeon
Adoptadane Rescue Qld. Inc
Nash, Gavin and Archie
Andrea and Vaughan
Eddie Church
Rex & Wilson
Pippa Belle
Mason & Zylee
Murrabit Group School
Charlotte Rose Egan
River and Judah
Lucky Trifilo
Makayla Mary Reid
Thomas
Quinton Nan Grosz
Ruby and Leo
Casey Foster
Angela and Elliott Warren
Lily Rayne Cockfield
Alexis Joan McKenner

Chenoa and Zaeli Cutter
Chanelle, Ruby and Jack Cutter
Les and Lynne Crichton
Zayden and Oliver
Brylea, Ava and Baby Fehring
Big Poppa
Fulton Family
Hannah
Tyler & Logan
Trixie
Ruby, Charlotte & Grace
Angus, Jigsaw (Jiggy) and Sweetie
Charlie
Delta and Pyp
Marli and Ollie
Kennedy
Ella
Tilly and Sam
Kaylah and Hayden
Jameson and Matthew
Kyan
Cadeyrn McLoughlan
Noah
Joshua and Lucas
Eden
Ruben
Alana and Hailey
Spencer and Lillian Walsh

30